# BERMUDA SHIPWRECKS

## By Daniel & Denise Berg

## A VACATIONING DIVER'S GUIDE
## TO
## BERMUDA'S SHIPWRECKS

*Foreword by Teddy Tucker*

Library of Congress Catalog Card No. 90-084836
ISBN: 0-9616167-4-1

FOR ADDITIONAL COPIES, WRITE TO:
**AQUA EXPLORERS, INC.**
**P.O. Box 116**
**East Rockway, N.Y. 11518**
Phone/Fax (516) 868-2658

Copyright © 1991

# FOREWORD

As sport diving has become the fastest growing of all water sports worldwide, with hotels and cruise ships catering solely to divers, this book is well timed and puts Bermuda in the limelight as one of the greastest diving sites accessible to the millions of divers living in the United States and Canada.

From the first quarter of the 16th century, Bermuda became a landmark for Spanish ships sailing back to Spain from the New World. The desire to sight Bermuda to confirm their position often ended their voyage as they wrecked on Bermuda's outer reefs. Bermuda collected more and more shipwrecks as voyages to the New World increased.

Dan and Denise Berg who researched many of these wrecks have made information readily available to the diving public. Through their vivid illustrations and informative text, the *Bermuda Shipwrecks* book has earned a place in every diver's library.

Edward B. (Teddy) Tucker
Treasure Hunter.
Maritime Historian.

Edward B. (Teddy) Tucker is one of the most accomplished and celebrated divers in the western world. Mr. Tucker has built an international reputation as an expert in armaments, shipbuilding and maritime history. Photo by Daniel Berg.

# ACKNOWLEDGEMENTS

We would like to thank the following for their time, knowledge, information and participation in this project. Christine Berg for editing and proof reading; Sonesta Beach Hotel for their hospitality, Bermuda Archives, Garrett Metal Detectors, Postmaster General Clevelyn Crichlow for allowing use of Bermuda Wreck series stamps; Chris Addams, Steve Bielenda, Ellsworth Boyd, Mel Brenner, Laura F. Brown, Michael Burke, Bill Campbell, Andrea Cordani, Mike Davis, Mike DeCamp, Ted Gosling, Professor Richard Gould, Jean Haviland, Peter Haynes, Brendan Hollis, Ann C. House, Steve Jonassen, Hank Keatts, Stephen Kerr, Gary Lamb, Alan Marquardt, Ian Murdoch, Peter Phillips, William Schell, Rick Schwarz, Jorma J. Sjoblom, John Stephenson, especially Edna and Teddy Tucker, and Professor Gordon Watts; last, but certainly not least, Winfred M. Berg, Donald Berg and Aaron Hirsh for all of their technical advice.

# UNDERWATER PHOTOGRAPHY

We would like to acknowledge and sincerely thank those who have donated their beautiful underwater photographs for this publication. It is these professionals who made this book possible. They are Michael Burke, Mike DeCamp, Stephen Kerr, Alan Marquardt, Peter Phillips and Teddy Tucker.

## SPECIAL NOTE

The removal of shipwreck artifacts in Bermuda is now restricted. The artifact photographs contained in this text were recovered before the new regulations went into effect.

*Divers should take nothing but photographs
and leave nothing but bubbles.*

# ABOUT THE AUTHORS

Photo By Mike Burke.

*Dan Berg is a P.A.D.I. (Professional Association of Diving Instructors) Master Scuba Diver Trainer. He is a Specialty Instructor in Wreck Diving, Night Diving, Search and Recovery, Underwater Hunting, Deep Diving, Dry Suit Diving, U/W Metal Detector Hunting, U/W Archeology, and has written and teaches his own nationally approved Distinctive Specialty courses in Shipwreck Research, Shipwreck Sketching and U/W Cinematography. Dan also holds certifications in Rescue and Environmental Marine Ecology. He is on the board of advisors and is an instructor for C.U.R.E. (Center for Underwater Research and Exploration) and is a member of the American Sport Divers Association. Dan is the author of the original WRECK VALLEY book, a record of shipwrecks off Long Island's South Shore; SHORE DIVER, a diver's guide to Long Island's beach sites; WRECK VALLEY Vol II, a record of shipwrecks off Long Island's South shore and New Jersey; co-author of TROPICAL SHIPWRECKS, a vacationing diver's guide to the Bahamas and Caribbean; publisher of the Wreck Valley LORAN C COORDINATE LIST, co-producer of the WRECK VALLEY VIDEO SERIES and SHIPWRECKS OF GRAND CAYMAN VIDEO. His award winning underwater cinematography has been used on a variety of TV and cable TV shows including LONG ISLAND ALL OUTDOORS, FOX 5 NEWS, CHANNEL 9 NEWS, CHANNEL 11 NEWS, LONG ISLAND FISHING, CBS NEWS, EYE WITNESS NEWS, NEWS 12 and DIVER'S DOWN. Dan's photographs and shipwreck articles have been published in SKIN DIVER MAGAZINE, UNDERWATER USA, NAUTICAL BRASS, The FISHERMAN MAGAZINE, FISHEYE VIEW MAGAZINE, SHIPWRECKS, NAUTILUS plus many more, and he is a contributing editor for the magazine SHIPWRECKS.*

*Denise Berg is a P.A.D.I. certified open water diver with specialty ratings in Underwater Photography, Equipment Maintenance, Shipwreck Research and is also a certified Regulator Repair Technician. Denise is co-author of TROPICAL SHIPWRECKS, has done modeling for nationally sold underwater videos, and has had her articles published in SKIN DIVER MAGAZINE, SHIPWRECKS and NAUTICAL BRASS.*

*Dan and Denise have made many wreck diving excursions. Avid wreck divers, both have always found Bermuda to contain some of the most historic and intriguing shallow water wreck diving anywhere in the world.*

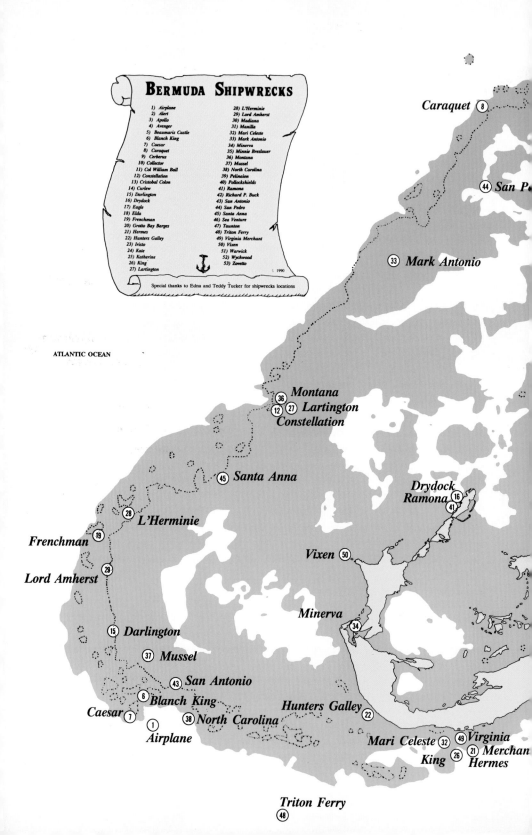

# BERMUDA SHIPWRECKS

1) Airplane
2) Alert
3) Apollo
4) Avenger
5) Beaumaris Castle
6) Blanch King
7) Caesar
8) Caraquet
9) Cerberus
10) Collector
11) Col William Ball
12) Constellation
13) Cristobal Colon
14) Curlew
15) Darlington
16) Drydock
17) Eagle
18) Elda
19) Frenchman
20) Grotto Bay Barges
21) Hermes
22) Hunters Galley
23) Iristo
24) Kate
25) Katherine
26) King
27) Lartington

28) L'Herminie
29) Lord Amherst
30) Madiana
31) Manilla
32) Mari Celeste
33) Mark Antonio
34) Minerva
35) Minnie Breslauer
36) Montana
37) Mussel
38) North Carolina
39) Pelinaion
40) Pollockshields
41) Ramona
42) Richard P. Buck
43) San Antonio
44) San Pedro
45) Santa Anna
46) Sea Venture
47) Taunton
48) Triton Ferry
49) Virginia Merchant
50) Vixen
51) Warwick
52) Wychwood
53) Zovetto

© 1990

Special thanks to Edna and Teddy Tucker for shipwrecks locations

ATLANTIC OCEAN

Caraquet (8)

(44) San P

(33) Mark Antonio

Montana
(36) (27) Lartington
(12) Constellation

(45) Santa Anna

Drydock
Ramona (16)
(41)

(28) L'Herminie

Frenchman (19)

Vixen (50)

Lord Amherst (29)

(15) Darlington

Minerva
(34)

(37) Mussel

(43) San Antonio

(6) Blanch King

Caesar (7)
(1)
(38) North Carolina
Airplane

Hunters Galley (22)

Mari Celeste (32) (49) Virginia
King (26) (21) Merchan
Hermes

Triton Ferry
(48)

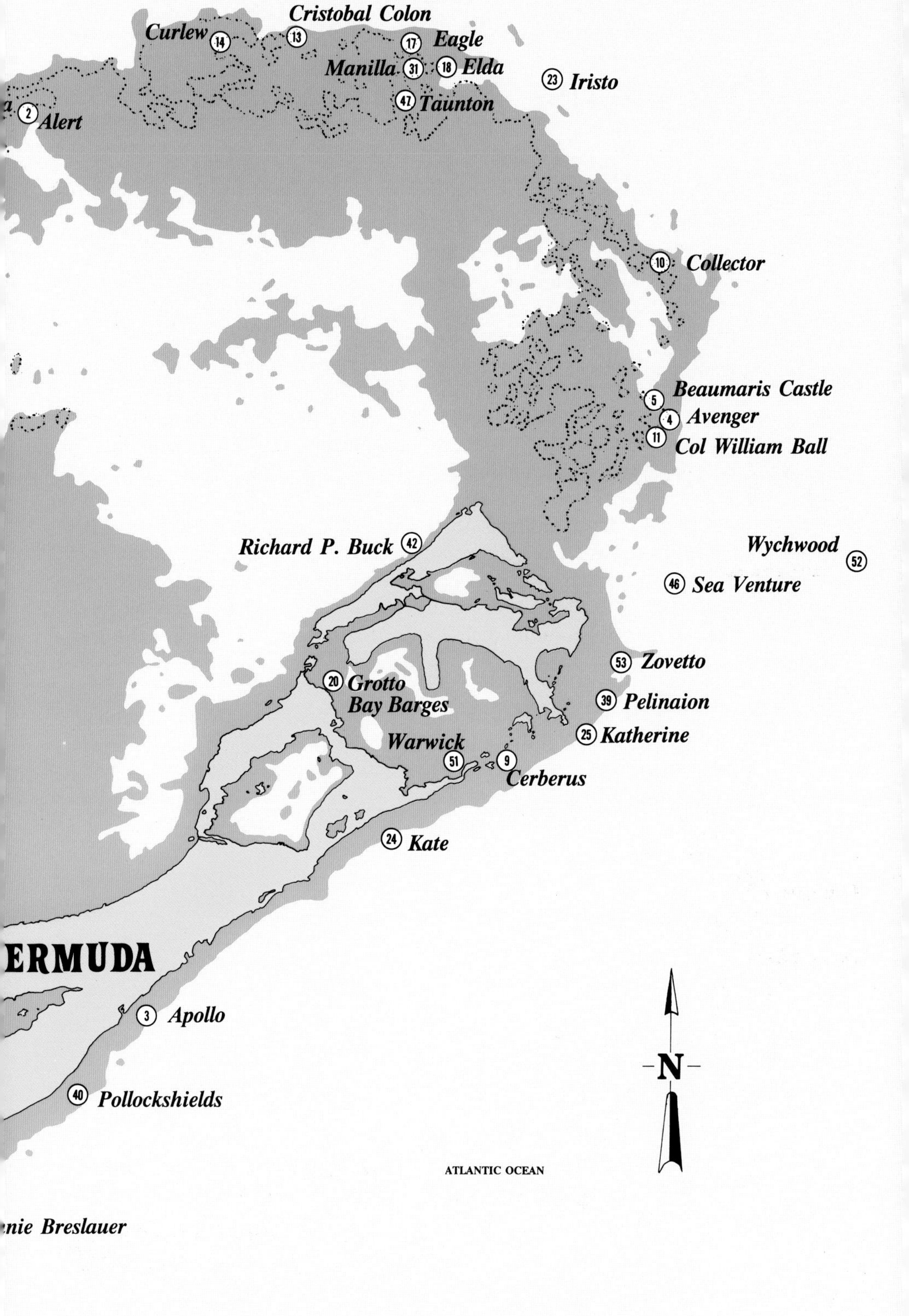
Cristobal Colon
Curlew
(14)
(13)
(17)
Eagle
Manilla
(31)
(18)
Elda
(23)
Iristo
(2)
Alert
(47)
Taunton
(10)
Collector
(5)
Beaumaris Castle
(4)
Avenger
(11)
Col William Ball
Richard P. Buck
(42)
Wychwood
(52)
(46)
Sea Venture
(53)
Zovetto
(20)
Grotto
Bay Barges
(39)
Pelinaion
(25)
Katherine
Warwick
(51)
(9)
Cerberus
(24)
Kate
ERMUDA
(3)
Apollo
N
(40)
Pollockshields
ATLANTIC OCEAN
nie Breslauer

# HOW TO USE

This text was designed to be a diver's, tourist's and marine historian's guide to shipwrecks located around Bermuda. Divers can easily reference this manual to find information about the history and present condition of over 55 of Bermuda's most popular shipwrecks. You will also find many photographs, including topside historical, underwater and artifact. Historical information in this guide will help you to have a better understanding of each wreck site. Note that many shipwrecks are known by two, three or even four different names. Some of these names were given to unidentified wrecks; some are the vessel's original name, which had been changed before the ship's sinking.

Bermuda's reefs have claimed thousands of ships and will probably continue to do so. We have chosen some of the more popular wrecks for this book. If you have information on other shipwrecks, located in Bermuda, that are being enjoyed by sport divers, please contact the publisher. We will be more then happy to update the text for future printings.

The easiest way to look up a particular wreck within this reference manual is to look up the name you have for the wreck in the index. We have tried to list all known names for the wrecks.

# AIRPLANE

The *Airplane* wreck's propeller.
Photo by Alan Marquardt.

Back around 1961, a U.S. B-29 *Bomber* that had taken off from Bermuda went down due to a fuel problem. Fortunately the crew was able to bail out before she hit the water, and all lives were spared.

Now known as the *Airplane* wreck, she lies in only 25 to 30 feet of water close to the wreck of the *North Carolina*. Divers can still recognize many of the plane's parts such as her propeller, wings and parts of her fuselage.

# ALERT

Bermuda wreck series postage stamp. Courtesy Postmaster General.

The Bermuda fishing sloop, *Alert*, was sunk in March of 1877. According to Teddy Tucker, a well known Bermudian maritime historian, the *Alert* had set out on a fishing trip and was not seen nor heard from again until a month later when she was found where she had sunk, amongst the north reef in 40 feet of water. All hands were lost with the ship.

# APOLLO

The American two masted wood schooner, *Apollo*, was built in Maine in 1873. According to her License of Vessel, she was 36 feet long, had a 14 foot beam, displaced 12 gross tons and was owned by William Elmello, of

Gloucester, Massachusetts. The schooner was bound from Turks Island to Nova Scotia under the command of Captain Jones, with a cargo of salt when she was wrecked on Bermuda's treacherous reefs in February of 1890. Today, the unidentified wreck known as *Apollo* lies scattered along Bermuda's south shore breakers in 20 feet of water.

# *AVENGER*

The English brigantine, *Avenger*, was bound from Nova Scotia to the West Indies when she became wrecked on the island of Bermuda in February of 1984. According to Teddy Tucker, a local treasure hunter, this ship was sailing under the command of Captain F.C. Hicks and was carrying a cargo of salt, fish and saw boards, when she smashed into Mills Breakers.

Today, there are a total of at least three wrecks resting on Mills Breakers which include the *Colonel William Ball*, *Beaumaris Castle* and *Avenger*.

# *BEAUMARIS CASTLE*

The English iron hulled sailing vessel, *Beaumaris Castle*, was built in Glasgow in 1864. She was 202 feet long had a 35.6 foot beam and displaced 1,040 tons. According to Lloyds register, she was owned by Merchant S.H. Company and was enroute from Calcutta, India, to New York when she ran aground on April 25, 1873. At the time, she was under the command of Captain Emmett and carrying a cargo of jute, linseed oil and gum. Although the weather was hazy, many local boats went to her assistance. These small boats could do little more than transport some of her cargo and crew to shore. Coast Wrecking Company of New York happened to be on the island at the time of this unfortunate incident and within a few weeks had placed their four powerful Worthington and two Andrews pumps into the *Beaumaris Castle's* hold. Each Worthington discharged 60 barrels of sea water per minute, and the Andrews pumped 30 barrels per minute, which should have made for a simple and fast salvage, but due to bad weather, salvage was delayed until June. During the early part of June, before the second attempt of raising the wreck, the salvage company suffered the tragic loss of one of their crew. Edward Ryan had gone deep into the *Beaumaris Castle's* hold to clear a clogged pump. He was immediately overcome by poison gas emitted from the decomposed cargo. Others, including Captain Brown, rushed to Ryan's aid but were also overcome by the foul gases. When all the bodies were finally recovered, Ryan, who had been exposed the longest, was dead. The three others recovered from the toxic poisoning. Shortly after this tragedy, the Wrecking Company decided to abandon their attempts to raise the vessel.

Today this wreck, which was originally identified by local marine historian, Michael Davis, can be found along with the wreck of the *Colonel William Ball* scattered atop of Mill's Breakers. Divers will find a row of dead eyes along her port side that mark the site. Her bow section points toward the surface on the northern side of the breaker in 25 feet of water.

# *BLANCH KING*

The American schooner, *Blanch King*, was built in 1887 by New England S.B. Company, Bath, Maine, for T.T. Anderson. She was 192 feet long, 42 feet wide and displaced 1,156 gross tons and 1,021 net tons. According to her Certificate of Registry, she had two decks, four masts, a Billet head and an Elliptic stern. During her career, she was sold five times. Her last owner was the U.S. Shipping Company.

The *Blanch King* was enroute from Norfolk to Bermuda under the command of Captain Pattison. On December 2, 1920, with a cargo of coal, she was stranded on the southwest reefs and sunk. At the time of her loss, she had eight crew men aboard; all got off safely.

This wreck now sits in 35 feet of water in a sand hole surrounded by shallow reefs. Cable and rigging are scattered across the surrounding reefs. Within her main wreckage is the center board box for her retractable keel. Divers will also notice some machinery and a capstan on the site.

Dead Eyes from the *Blanch King's* rigging.
Photo by Daniel Berg.

The author Daniel Berg holds a Dead Eye he recovered from the *Blanch King*.
Photo by Stephen Kerr.

11

# *CAESAR*

Bermuda wreck series
postage stamps. Courtesy
Postmaster General.

The English brig, *Caesar*, was built at Cumberland, Co., Durham, in 1814. On May 17, 1818, while enroute from Shields, England, to Baltimore, she was wrecked on a Bermuda reef. The following is taken from Lloyd's List of July 3, 1818. "The *Caesar*, Richardson, of and from Newcastle to Baltimore, was lost on a reef of rocks off the West End of Bermuda on 17th May. Part of the cargo saved with damage. Spars, rigging etc. also saved." At the time of her demise, she was under the command of Captain James Richardson, with a crew of seven and a cargo of grindstones, medicine vials, decorated flasks, grandfather clock parts, glassware, white, red and black lead oxide, and a marble cornice for a Baltimore church.

The *Caesar's* cargo of grindstones lay in a sand hole in 35 feet of water.
Photo by Daniel Berg.

The author Daniel Berg searches the *Caesar* wreck area with a Garrett Sea Hunter XL500 metal detector. Photo by Mike Burke.

Divers dredge deep holes in search
of finding one of the rare bottles
the *Caesar* carried as part of her
cargo. Photo courtesy Peter Phillips.

Broken bottles from the *Caesar*.
Photo by Daniel Berg.

Two beautiful antique bottles recovered from
the *Caesar* by Teddy Tucker. Look closely and
you will notice that the bottles are standing on
grindstones, also from the wreck. Teddy has
made a stone path in his backyard from these
grindstones. Photo by Daniel Berg.

This wreck was salvaged by Teddy Tucker, but even today divers will still find large grindstones, glassware and bottles on the site. She rests in a 35 foot deep sand pocket on the southwest side of the island.

# *CARAQUET*

The British mail steamship, *Caraquet*, was built for Union S.S. Company, Ltd., Southampton, as the *Guelph* in 1894 by Harland & Wolf, Ltd., Belfast. She was later sold in 1913 to the Royal Mail Steam Packet Company, London, and re-named *Caraquet*.

The British mail steamship *Caraquet*. Photo courtesy Steamship Historical Society.

Wreck series postage stamp.

On June 25, 1923, under the command of Captain Fernandez, on a voyage from St. John to Halifax, carrying passengers and general cargo, this fine ship was wrecked on Bermuda's treacherous northern barrier reef. Captain Fernandez had trouble pinpointing his vessel's exact location due to an increasingly rough sea and a misty fog. He had calculated his position to be farther north when the *Caraquet* smashed violently into the reef, just west of North Rock. All passengers, crew and mail were landed safely without mishap, and her cargo was later salvaged.

The Marine Board of Inquiry investigating the incident determined that an abnormally strong current had pushed the *Caraquet* further than Captain Fernandez had calculated. He was exonerated of any blame.

Diver explores the wreck of the British mail steamship *Caraquet* which was sunk in 1923.
Photo courtesy Mike DeCamp.

The *Caraquet* is smashed up and laid out in 30 to 45 feet of water ten miles north of Hamilton. According to Teddy Tucker, her wreckage is spread over a good two acres of the ocean floor. Teddy recovered her bronze propeller among other artifacts from the site. Divers will still recognize her four enormous boilers, deck plates, capstans, winches, massive anchor, lots of lead pipe and her propellers.

# H.M.S. CERBERUS

The *H.M.S. Cerberus* was a 5th Rate 32 gun ship of 701 bm (an early measurement of tonnage). She was 126 feet long, 35.5 feet wide and was built by Randall at Rotherhithe. The *Cerberus* was launched on June 15, 1779.

Researcher Andrea Cordani was able to trace down some clues to the cause of the *Cerberus* sinking. She found a reference in the book ADMIRALTY LIST OF SHIPS LOST 1759-1815, about a midshipman's lost pay book. It states that the midshipman, "served till 21 February 1783 at which time *Cerberus* was lost coming out of Castle Harbour in the Island of Bermuda..." After a little more research, we found other references that told us that the officers and crew of the *Cerberus* went aboard the French prize, La Sybil, and that Sir Jacob Wheate, Captain of the *Cerberus*, later contracted fever and died in February 1783. A court martial was held on October 18, 1783, on board the H.M.S. Dictator. Gunner H. Shrewsbury reported that the pilot had come aboard and ordered the ship unmoor'd. A few minutes after passing the Castle, the ship struck the rocks. His statement continues about unsuccessful action taken to save the ship, including cutting the masts away and throwing guns and shot overboard. The crew was then ordered to abandon ship and were taken to the castle. The ship had water up to the ports. In days following the sinking, the crew did manage to salvage some guns and carriages. Due to the loss of the *Cerberus*, the Admiralty forbade the further use of Castle Harbour as an anchorage for H.M. Ships.

According to Mike Davis, this wreck is also known as the *Musket Ball Wreck* simply due to the abundance of balls found on the site.

## COLLECTOR

The American schooner, *Collector*, sailing under the command of Captain Hall, was enroute from St. John's, New Brunswick, to Bermuda and South America, when she was wrecked on May 26, 1823. At the time of her sinking, she had a general cargo in her hold.

## COLONEL WILLIAM G. BALL

The luxury yacht, *Colonel William G. Ball* was built in 1929 by George Lawley & Son, Neponset, Massachusetts. She was originally named *Sialia* and later renamed *Egeria*. She was 119.4 feet long, had a 23 foot

Luxury yacht *Colonel William G. Ball*. Photo courtesy Mike Davis.

16

The *Colonel William Ball* sinking bow first in 1943. Photo courtesy Brendan Hollis collection.

beam and displaced 291 gross tons. In 1941, she was re-named again when taken over by the U.S. Army Transportation Corps and commissioned as a harbor boat.

In June, 1943, the *Colonel William G. Ball*, while under the command of Captain Fred Anderson, was wrecked on Mills Breakers, a shallow reef, while returning to port during severe weather. The ship was a total loss.

The Army investigated the incident, and it was discovered that a marker buoy used to warn vessels of shallow water had broken free of its mooring.

Today, the wreck of the *William G. Ball* sits in 15 to 26 feet of water on Mills Breakers beside the wreck of the *Beaumaris Castle*.

## CONSTELLATION

The four masted schooner, *Constellation*, was built in 1918 by Frye Flinn Company in Harrington, Maine. She was originally named *Sally Persis Noyes* and sailed as part of the Crowell and Thurlow fleet. She was later sold in 1932 to Robert L. Royall and renamed *Constellation*. Mr Royall's plan was to refit this fine sailing ship and make her into a floating nautical school. She was completely rebuilt and provided with all of the modern

The four masted schooner *Constellation*. Photo courtesy South Street Seaport Museum Collection.

comforts, including electricity, refrigeration, plumbing, a modern galley and large staterooms. Unfortunately, Mr. Royall's plans did not work. It seemed that there was little interest in this type of sailing, and within a year the ship was put up for sale. The *Constellation* found her way to New York and after one or two short trips remained there until 1942. When World War II was in full fury, the demand for ships of any kind was enormous. The *Constellation*, now owned by Intercontinental S.S. Company, was converted back into a cargo vessel.

In the late spring of 1942, the *Constellation* set sail on her first voyage since being reconverted. Carrying a 2,000 ton general cargo, including hundreds of bags of cement, 700 cases of Scotch whiskey, and an assortment of drugs, she was en-route from New York to La Guira, Venezuela. Not long after clearing New York, her steam pumping gear broke down, and she began to take on water from the increasingly rough weather. The crew used

Wreck series postage stamp of the *Constellation*. Courtesy Postmaster General.

The *Constellation* deck cargo of cement bags has now hardened to become a small mountain in the sand. Photo by Alan Marquardt.

The *Constellation* was carrying thousands of drug ampuls when she sank on July 30, 1942. Photo by Daniel Berg.

Lead crucifix recovered from the *Constellation* by Teddy Tucker. Photo by Daniel Berg.

The author Denise Berg holds a drug ampul and china cup she found on the wreck. Photo by Daniel Berg.

19

hand pumps for several days but could not keep up with the leaking schooner. Captain Howard Neaves, who was 71 years of age, headed toward Bermuda for repairs. On July 30, 1942, while waiting for a local pilot, during a flat calm, sea, she was driven onto a reef by the strong current. The ship was a total loss, but the United States Navy managed to save some of her cargo including the 700 cases of Scotch.

In the mid 1970's, Peter Benchley wrote an adventure story called THE DEEP. It was the *Constellation* that was the model for his best selling novel and later the multi-million dollar motion picture, starring Jacqueline Bisset, Nick Nolte and Robert Shaw. Amongst her general cargo, the *Constellation* had carried thousands of drug ampuls full of adrenaline, anti-tetanus serum, opium, morphine, and penicillin. There is a second wreck on the site, the *Montana*. Benchley used both of these oddities to enhance his best selling novel and acclaimed film. He also based Robert Shaw's character, Romer Treece, on the world famous Bermudian treasure hunter, Teddy Tucker.

Today, the wreck of the *Constellation*, also commonly known as the *Woolworth Wreck*, sits on a sand and coral bottom in 25 to 30 feet of water. She is completely broken up and scattered over a large area. Divers will note a huge pile of cement bags, now hardened, piled into a small mountain in the sand. This was part of her deck cargo, and divers have found everything from tennis rackets, coffee cups, nail polish bottles, ceramic tiles, bottles, lead crucifixes, yo-yos and drug ampuls in and around this area.

Within easy swimming distance of about 50 feet is the wreck of the *Montana*, which went down in 1863. In fact, an untrained eye could easily confuse both wrecks as one.

# CRISTOBAL COLON

The Spanish luxury liner, *Cristobal Colon*, was built for the Trasatlantica Spanish Line by Soc Espanola de Const. Naval, El Ferrol in 1923. She was 499.4 feet long, had a 61 foot beam, displaced 10,833 gross tons and was one of the most luxurious cruise ships of her time.

On October 25, 1936, the *Cristobal Colon*, under the command of Captain Crescencia Narvarrro Delgado, ran high on a reef while steaming at 15 knots east of North Rock, eight miles north of Bermuda. At the time, she was travelling in ballast with no passengers, but with 160 crew members, from Cardiff, Wales, to Vera Cruz, Mexico. Captain Crescencia Narvarro testified later that he came close to Bermuda to check his instruments by

Spanish luxury liner *Cristobal Colon.* Photo courtesy Steamship Historical Society Collection.

light. According to the NEW YORK TIMES, "He sighted a fixed light, which he believed to be St. David's and later a close blinking light, which he believed to be the North Rock Beacon. He altered his course and said the wreck was caused because North Rock was not lighted, which fact the authorities here advertised months ago." North Rock Light had been out since October 18th, repairs being prevented by bad weather.

This vessel had a very interesting history in the weeks prior to her

21

## Cristobal Colon

The *Cristobal Colon* was 499.4 feet long and displaced 10,833 gross tons. Photo courtesy Steamship Historical Society Collection.

destruction on Bermuda's reefs. It seems that this Spanish ship was originally enroute from Mexico to Vigo, Spain, with 344 passengers aboard. When the Spanish Civil War broke out, she was not permitted into port because Vigo was under control of the rebels. Her passengers were not permitted to land at Southampton, England, either, and she was ordered to France. French authorities would not permit the landing of Spaniards, so the *Cristobal Colon* anchored in St. Nazaire awaiting further orders. On August 15th, a leftist crew took command of the ship. Some passengers were permitted to disembark at Nates, France, before the *Colon* sailed for the Spanish harbor, Santander. There are many who believe that the *Cristobal Colon* was steaming to Mexico to pick up arms for Spain's war effort.

The crew from the wrecked cruise ship found bad luck waiting for them ashore as well. It seems that Bermudians disliked them because they could not understand them. The Government also feared that Bermuda would have to pay for their food and housing. The Spanish Government ignored Bermuda's distressed communications about the crew. Mexico refused to take any responsibility for their welfare as did Cuba and France. Bermuda's government, realizing that the un-welcome guests would be with them for a while, put the men to work. They repaired Barry Road and restored Gates

The wreck of the *Cristobal Colon* sitting high on a reef. Note the life boats and assisting vessel in the area. Photo courtesy Mike Davis colection.

Fort. Finally on Christmas Eve, the Spaniards boarded the Reina del Pacifico for La Pallice, France, where they then boarded a train for their homeland. Some sources claim that they were all executed upon their return by the Franco government.

The wreck of the *Cristobal Colon* sat high on the reef only eight miles from Dockyard for some time. This allowed for the easy salvage of some of her fine furniture, paintings and fittings. In fact, many homes in Bermuda are still adorned with items from the wreck. Many of these articles were bought at public auction, while others were taken in the age old Bermudian custom of piracy. Each night motor boats filled with loot from the luxurious ship would return to the island under the cover of darkness. Literally hundreds of Bermudians took part in this modern day piracy; only 13 were ever caught, and of those twelve were convicted.

In 1937, Captain Stephensen of the Norwegian steamer, *Iristo*, seeing the *Cristobal Colon*, which appeared to be a perfectly sound ship under way in a channel, made the tragic mistake of following her. The Iristo soon found her hull being ripped open by the shallow reefs. After this incident, the Marine Court of Inquiry had the *Colon's* funnel and mast removed in hopes that the slightly disfigured wreck would not lure any other vessels into the reefs.

In the early 1940's the *Cristobal Colon* was used as a target by the American

23

One of the *Cristobal Colon's* spare propellers. Photo by Mike Burke.

Divers work on recovering a porthole from one of the *Colon's* hull plates. Photo by Mike DeCamp.

Divers can still see an unexploded artillery shell on the wreck. Photo courtesy Mike DeCamp.

John Stephenson holds a porthole he recovered from the *Cristobal Colon*. Photo by Daniel Berg.

Silverware from the *Cristobal Colon* which was bought at public auction. Courtesy Edna and Teddy Tucker, Photo by Dan Berg.

Air Force for bombing practice, so she is now completely blown apart and scattered over a huge area.

Today the *Cristobal Colon*, the largest shipwreck in Bermuda, lies split in two with half of her wreck on one side of the reef and half on the other. Divers can still see an unexploded artillery shell on the wreck. Her eight massive coal burning boilers, two spare propellers and deck winches are easily recognizable. Depth at this site ranges from 15 feet in the bow to 60 feet in the stern; a depth of 80 feet can be reached in the sand off her stern.

# *CURLEW*

The iron hulled three masted, English steamer, *Curlew*, was Barquentine rigged and poop deck fitted. She was 182 feet in length, had a 22 foot beam and displaced 528 gross tons. She was purchased by the Cunard Steamship company on July 20, 1853, and regularly sailed the Halifax-Bermuda-St. Thomas run.

On March 14, 1856, she left Halifax under the command of Captain

Wreck series postage stamp of the *Curlew*. Courtesy Postmaster General.

Hunter. According to marine historian Mike Davis, Captain Hunter was below deck sleeping on that Monday morning of the 17th, after having spent all night steering his ship through rough seas. The Captain awoke to find his ship had struck the northern reefs of Bermuda. The *Curlew* was soon to be doomed; her cabin quickly filled with sea water. Two of her life boats were smashed while attempting to launch them, and a third drifted away. The fourth boat was successfully launched, and it was decided that the officers would stay aboard the steamer while the others would row the lifeboat to shore and then send help. Two Navy ships quickly went to the sinking vessel's assistance. They saved not only the men, who by this time had been forced into the rigging, but also seven of the nine mail bags she had carried.

Teddy Tucker originally located and identified this scattered wreckage located one mile east of North Rock in 35 feet of water. He recovered some brass fittings and some assorted artifacts from her broken bones.

# *DARLINGTON*

The steel hulled English steamer, *Darlington*, was built in 1881 by Swan & Hunter, Newcastle, for W. Milburn & Company, London, She was 285.5 feet in length, had a 36 foot beam, displaced 1,990 gross tons and was powered by 250 h.p. compound inverted engines.

On February 22, 1886, the *Darlington* was wrecked on Western Reef, while on a voyage from New Orleans to Bremen, Germany, carrying a cargo of 5,152 bales of cotton and 15,000 bushels of grain. According to the NEW YORK TIMES, "Captain Richard Ward of the *Darlington* made some error in calculating her position, and she struck on the reefs early in the morning".

Captain Ward was later found negligent by the Marine Board of Inquiry for failure to post a lookout while approaching the unfamiliar waters of Bermuda.

The *Darlington's* crew of 23 and five officers were transported back to New York aboard the steamship Orinoco.

The *Darlington's* propeller. Photo by Mike DeCamp.

Today, the wreck lies off the west end in shallow water about 15 to 30 feet. She remains fairly intact but has collapsed onto herself and lies on her port side. Her rudder quadrant still breaks the surface in heavy weather, and her boilers, winches and propeller shaft are easily recognizable. Within swimming distance of the *Darlington* are the buried remains of an unidentified Spanish Galleon.

# DRYDOCK

This huge old drydock was deliberately sunk in an area Teddy Tucker refers to as the junk yard. After she was of no more use because of her age, she was towed about 300 yards offshore and sunk in 60 feet of water. Teddy goes on to say that this area has been used as a dump site since the mid 19th century. Mike Burke told us that this wreck sits upright and that the bow of the *Ramona*, a Canadian yacht dumped here in 1968, actually sits inside this old drydock.

# EAGLE

The English merchantman, *Eagle*, was owned by the Virginia Company and under the command of Captain George Withy when she was wrecked on the northeast breakers on Jan 12, 1659. At the time, she was on a voyage from Plymouth, England, to Jamestown, Virginia, carrying passengers and cargo. Her crew took to life boats and made it to shore safely.

This wreck was originally discovered in 1956 quite by chance when the yacht, *Elda*, wrecked almost on top of her. The *Eagle* has been salvaged by Teddy Tucker. She sits in a large sand hole in 35 feet of water by the North East Breakers. Teddy has recovered clay pipes, pewter spoons, flint ballast, candle sticks and a variety of 17th century artifacts from the site. Today, not much is left of the *Eagle*, but divers can still observe two cannons on the site.

# EARLY RISER

Wreck series postage stamp of the *Early Riser*. Courtesy Postmaster General.

The *Early Riser* was an eight oared, two masted sailing pilot boat. According to Teddy Tucker, the wreck of the *Early Riser*, which is pictured on a Bermuda postage stamp, has never been located. The *Early Riser* sank back in 1876.

# ELDA

The yacht *Elda* sinking. Note the life raft and survivors in her stern. Photo courtesy Mike Davis collection.

The American yacht, *Elda*, was designed by Philp L. Rhodes and built in 1937 by Anderson & Combs, Inc. New Haven, Connecticut. She was owned by Paul Patterson, was 46 feet long, had an eleven foot beam and was based out of Gibson Island, Maryland.

On June 20, 1956, she was wrecked while racing from Newport to Bermuda.

The *Elda* now rests in shallow water very close to the *Eagle* wreck, an English merchantmen sunk in 1658. Her 6,000 pound lead keel and small engine are still visible on the site.

# *FRENCHMAN*

This unidentified shipwreck was found in 1983 by Bill McCallan. For the past few years, treasure hunter, Teddy Tucker, has been working the 60 foot deep site and recovering a vast array of artifacts that date back to the Revolutionary War period. The *Frenchman* also carried a cargo of wood. Teddy has recovered mahogany boards, probably for the furniture trade, and stacks of lignumvitae. Teddy also reports that there are ten cannons at the site and estimates that the wreck dates back to around 1750.

Teddy Tucker uses an airlift to uncover artifacts from the unidentified wreck known as *Frenchman*. Photos courtesy Edna and Teddy Tucker.

# GROTTO BAY BARGES

Within easy swimming distance from shore, rest the remains of three intact barges sitting upright in 15 feet of water. We have not been able to find any historical information on these little wrecks, but rumor has it that this area was used as a dump site, and these barges were scuttled deliberately. However they ended up here, these little wrecks are ideal for snorkeling.

# HERMES

This 165 foot long, 254 ton freighter was built in Pennsylvania in 1943. Originally a U.S. Navy buoy tender, she broke down while transporting a cargo of second hand gifts to poor families in the Cape Verde Islands. She was later abandoned in Bermuda because she had become too costly to repair. The government originally tried to sell the vessel to an American, but after he inspected the rusting ship, he promptly asked for the return of his $10,000 deposit. After some time, the government donated the rusting vessel to the Bermuda Divers Association (BDA). After being stripped and cleaned at Dockyard, she was scuttled on May 15, 1984, as a dive site one mile off shore by the Bermuda Divers Association (BDA). The *Hermes* has become one of the most popular wreck dives on the south side of the island. Unlike many wrecks lost to Bermuda's treacherous barrier reefs that are scattered across the sea bed, the *Hermes* is the classic story book shipwreck. She remains intact, upright and magnificently photogenic. She sits in 75 to 80 feet of water, and divers can explore her pilot house, galley, engine room and cargo hold. All of her hatches were removed prior to the ship's sinking to ensure safe wreck penetration.

The 165 foot long freighter *Hermes* was sunk by the Bermuda Divers Association on May 15, 1984. Photos by Alan Marquardt.

The *Hermes* has become a classic story book shipwreck. She remains intact, upright and magnificently photogenic. Photo by Michael Burke.

All of her hatches were removed prior to the ships sinking to ensure safe wreck penetration. Photo by Michael Burke.

The *Hermes* spot light. Photo courtesy Michael Burke.

31

# HUNTERS GALLEY

The American sailing sloop, *Hunters Galley*, was wrecked off the island of Bermuda during a gale on January 11, 1752. At the time, she was on a voyage from St. Eustatius to South Carolina under the command of Captain Clement Conyers with a general cargo.

The *Hunters Galley* did not founder as a result of just one storm. In fact, the ill fated ship suffered through three. During their journey, the vessel's rigging and sails had been severely damaged by a violent storm which also washed one crew man overboard. Captain Conyers decided to head to Bermuda for repairs. On January 9th, another hard gale hit, this time splitting her sails and rendering them almost useless. On the 10th, the crew spotted Bermuda. Captain Conyers anchored his vessel in Hogfish cut because the damaged ship could not be navigated into the harbor. On January 11, 1752, the vessel was washed onto the rocks by yet another of a series of gales.

Today, all that remains of this wreck, which lies 200 yards offshore of Pompano Beach in 12 feet of water, is some ballast and timbers on a sand bottom. Teddy Tucker, who originally located this wreck, told us that descendants of Captain Conyers still live in Bermuda.

# IRISTO

The Norwegian steamer, *Iristo*, was built in 1918 by American S.B. Company, Lorain, Ohio. Originally named *Lake Jessup*, she was 251 feet long, had a 43.5 foot beam and displaced 1,821 gross tons. This vessel was going to be named *War Briar* and was contracted to be built by the British Government. However, when the United States entered World War I, all merchant ships being built in the U.S. were requisitioned by the U.S. Shipping Board. She was sold in 1921 to the International Coal Transportation Corp. She was sold again in 1925 to Norwegian owners and re-named *Ekstrand*. She was again sold in 1935 to Hans F. Grann and re-named *Iristo*.

On March 15, 1937, under the command of Captain Christian Stephensen, she was enroute from St. John's, Newfoundland, to Bermuda, with a cargo of flour, 200 barrels of gasoline, a steam roller and a fire engine. Captain Christian spotted the *Cristobal Colon*, a ship that had run aground the year before and was sitting high on the submerged reef, and assumed she was under way and in the channel, even though the *Colon's* wreck information

The Norwegian steamer *Iristo* now sits in 50 to 55 feet of water. Photo by Alan Marquardt.

had been posted in Notice to Mariners. He ordered a change of course and actually followed the *Cristobal Colon* into the reefs about two miles off North Rock. She was pulled off at about 4:00 PM the same day by a salvage tug from St. George's. The next day, while in tow, the *Iristo* sunk one mile east of the North East Breakers to her final resting place due to the wounds she had suffered on the reef.

Captain Stephensen was blamed for the wreck by the Marine Board of Inquiry. He was charged with negligence for having no local charts or the knowledge published in the Notice to Mariners about the year old *Cristobal Colon* wreck.

This wreck is known locally as the *Aristo*. This spelling may have come from the original NEW YORK TIMES report on the wreck in which reporters misspelled her name.

Today, the *Iristo* is resting very close to the *Cristobal Colon* wreck on a sand and coral bottom in 50 to 55 feet of water. Her stern and bow are intact, and divers will find two large anchors, her boilers, engine and a broken propeller that all make for excellent photo opportunities.

## KATE

The English iron steamer, *Kate*, was built in Whitby, England in 1874. She was approximately 200 feet long, displaced 1,413 tons and was enroute from Galveston, Texas to La Harve, France, under the command of Captain James Simpson. On November 30, 1878, with 3,602 bales of cotton in her holds, the *Kate* struck an unknown reef 22 miles northwest of Gibbs Hill lighthouse. Soon after this incident, the vessel also hit Long Bar and began to take on water. Captain Simpson summoned assistance, and the *Kate* was soon taken in tow by the tugboat, Ackerman. Due to the extensive damage suffered, the *Kate* had to be grounded in an attempt to prevent her from sinking. Salvage operations were commenced and approximately 120 bales of cotton were saved. On December 10th, a gale broke the *Kate* up considerably and blew her remains into deeper water. Almost 3,500 bales of cotton were recovered during a salvage operation that took place soon after the accident.

The *Kate's* propeller and shaft. Photo by Alan Marquardt.

Today the *Kate* sits in 45 feet of water. Her boilers, engine, propeller shaft and deck winches are all easily recognizable. Divers can also find her propeller sitting alone on top of the reef in 20 feet of water.

## KATHERINE

The English brigantine, *Katherine*, sunk on April 4, 1763. According to

Lloyd's List, June 21, 1763, "The *Katherine*, Simondson, of Liverpool from Philadelphia for Jamaica, was lost on the 4th of April on a rock near Bermudas, and the master, two passengers, one seaman and a boy were drowned." At the time of her demise, she was under the command of Captain Simondson.

Today, on the wreck site known as the *Katherine*, all that remains are some ballast and timbers.

# *KING*

The old Navy diesel powered tug boat, *King*, was built in South Carolina in 1941. She was 55 feet in length, had a 12.6 foot beam and was brought to Bermuda and converted into a treasure salvage vessel. Peter Haynes reports that she was later converted into a dive boat owned by Gary Lamb. Peter remembers the *King* having its own compressor and cascade system on board for filling scuba tanks.

In 1984 the *King* was donated by Gary Lamb and intentionally sunk as a dive site by South Side Scuba. She was the first vessel to be scuttled in Bermuda as a dive site and artificial reef. Her success at attracting fish and satisfying divers has encouraged other ventures like the sinking of the *Hermes*, another popular scuttled shipwreck, and the ferry *Triton*.

According to Alan Marquardt, the *King* now sits intact with a 45 degree starboard list in 65 feet of water only one half mile off the south shore. She rests with her stern in the sand and her bow on a coral bottom. Divers can explore her pilot house and galley and even peer into her engine room. This little tug makes an excellent background for photographs.

The old navy tug *King* now sits in 65 feet of water. Photos by Alan Marquardt.

# LA BERMUDA

It is said that the island, Bermuda, was named after the Spanish ship, *La Bermuda*, which wrecked on the island's reefs around 1508. Other sources claim the name came from the Spaniard Juan Bermudez, who is believed to have discovered the island. Whatever the origin, the name Bermuda is certainly much more appropriate than "Isle of the Devils", a name used by sailors before the island was officially named. Unfortunately, the wreck of the *La Bermuda*, if it really exists, has yet to be located.

# LARTINGTON

This wreck has intrigued us for many years. When John Stephenson first took us to this site, he told of how the name *Lartington* could be read on the bottom port side of her bow. We thought this would be an easy wreck to research but soon found that there was no reference to a ship with this name in our usual sources of information. Fortunately, our friend, the noted ship historian, Bill Schell, found the following information in his files.

The *Lartington* was launched in June of 1875, by Short Brothers, Sunderland, England. She was owned by J.S. Barwick, was 245.1 feet in length, had a 32 foot beam and displaced 878 net tons. According to the Liverpool Underwriters Register, she was "wrecked on the Bermudas" in 1879.

After further research, Mike Davis, a local marine historian, was kind enough to give us his file on the wreck. Mike reports that the *Lartington* departed from Savannah on December 8th, with a full cargo of 4,000 bales of cotton. She was under the command of Captain George Dixon and bound for the port of Revel in Russia. A strong south easterly gale hit and washed away everything that wasn't tied down. At 8:00 AM on the 10th, the wind veered to the west. A huge sea struck the *Lartington's* stern causing a loud crack. Sea water started to pour in and although her pumps ran for ten hours, they could not keep up with the flooding water. On the 12th, Captain Dixon, fearing that his ship would founder, headed for Bermuda. On the morning of the 14th, 1878, the *Lartington* went aground near Western Blue Cut. The crew abandoned ship in lifeboats and was soon spotted and towed into Hamilton by a pilot boat.

The Marine Board of Inquiry attributed the stranding to gross negligence

The author Denise Berg explores the *Lartington's* stern. Photo by Daniel Berg.

The name *Lartington* can still be read on the bottom port side of her bow. Photo by Daniel Berg.

and carelessness. The Captain should have taken soundings for depth and should never have altered his course to the southeast.

For many years, before divers located the name *Lartington* on the bow of this wreck, there had been much confusion as to her identity. Many incorrectly referred to this wreck as the *Nola*. The *Nola* is one of the names used by the blockade runner, *Montana*, which sunk in 1863. Mike Davis was the first to suspect that something was wrong. His research brought him to believe that this wreck was the *Lartington*. This speculation was, of course, confirmed when her bow letters were found.

This wreck is broken down and scattered in 15 to 30 feet of water. She still lies in a straight line. Her bow is intact and lies on its port side. Amidships are her boilers, and in the stern section, divers will see her broken propeller. This wreck is excellent for underwater photography.

# *L'HERMINIE*

The 300 foot long French frigate *L'Herminie* sunk in 1838. Photo courtesy Mike Davis collection.

The 300 foot long, 60 gun French frigate, *L'Herminie*, was launched in 1824, and completed in 1828. She had been part of a Squadron in Mexican waters sent in order to enforce French claims against Mexico. The *L'Herminie* arrived in Havana on August 3,1837. Within three months, 133 of her crew came down with yellow fever. Since the *L'Herminie's* crew would be useless in battle, it was decided to recall her to France. On December 3, 1838, under the command of Commodore Bazoch, she was homeward bound from Havana to Brest, France. Due to rough weather Captain Bazoche headed for the shelter of Bermuda. By the time land was spotted, it was too late. The big ship was already inside Bermuda's reef structure and was doomed. Local boats came to her assistance and all 495 officers and crew were landed safely in Ely's Harbour.

Wreck series postage stamp of the *L'Herminie*. Courtesy
Postmaster General.

The most famous spot on this wreck are her two crossed cannons,
which have become a favorite for underwater photographers.
Photo by Alan Marquardt.

Teddy Tucker displays two projectiles he
recovered from the *L'Herminie* wreck.
Photo by Daniel Berg.

Teddy Tucker recovered the bell from the
*L'Herminie*. Photo courtesy Mike Davis
collection.

Some of the *L'Herminie's* stores were salvaged the next day. The crew departed Bermuda at the end of the month aboard the vessels, Hercules, Jean and Osage.

Today, the wreck of the *L'Herminie* is resting four miles west of Ireland Island in 30 to 35 feet of water on a sand and coral bottom. According to Mike Burke, divers can count 40 of her cannons on the sea bed, and those with a sharp eye may even see cannon balls. The most famous spot on this wreck are her two crossed cannons, which have become a favorite for underwater photographers. Divers will also see a huge fluted anchor on the site.

# LORD AMHERST

Wreck series postage stamp of the *Lord Amherst*. Courtesy Postmaster General.

The 24 gun English armed transport, *Lord Amherst*, has proved to be an elusive vessel to research. Lloyds List did not survive for the year 1778, and indexes to the LONDON TIMES do not start until 1785. We also found no listing of her in printed sources for the Navy. Treasure hunter, Teddy Tucker, in his wreck map of Bermuda, lists her as being wrecked on February 16, 1778. Teddy goes on to say that she was enroute from Jamaica to London, under the command of Captain Francis John Hartwell. She was being used as a hospital ship to carry injured sailors from the Revolutionary War back to England.

Today, the *Lord Amherst* sits on a western reef in 20 feet of water just south of the *L'Herminie*.

# MADIANA

The iron hulled Canadian passenger steamship, *Madiana*, was built by R. Napier & Sons, Glasgow, in 1877, as the *Balmoral Castle*. She was 344.8 feet long, had a 39.4 foot beam, displaced 3,080 gross tons and was powered by 383 n.p.h. triple expansion engines. She was sold in 1882 to Spanish owners and re-named *San Augustin*. Later she was sold to another British owner and reverted to *Balmoral Castle*. In the early 1890's, she was

Postage stamps of the *Madiana*. Courtesy Postmaster General.

purchased by the Quebec S.S. Company, Ltd., Montreal, and once again re-named *Madiana*.

On February 10, 1903, under command of Captain Roderick Frazer, while enroute from New York to the West Indies, with passengers and a general cargo, the *Madiana* went ashore on the reefs of Bermuda. According to reports from passengers, the *Madiana* was threading her way through the narrow channel along the coral reefs which lead to Hamilton Harbor, when she struck a reef northeast of North Rock. Distress signals were sent up, and tugs were sent to render assistance. The tug, Gladisfen, dared not approach the wreck due to a heavy sea and was forced to wait about a mile off. The *Madiana's* crew launched a life boat, but it was smashed to pieces against the steamer's side. Another boat was lowered into the threatening sea, this time successfully. Other lifeboats were then launched in succession, and all passengers and crew, after a long row through enormous seas finally reached safety aboard the awaiting Gladisfen.

The *Madiana*, on left, was an iron hulled passenger steamship that sunk in 1903. Photo courtesy Steamship Historical Society Collection.

The wreck of the *Madiana* was partially salvaged. Photo courtesy Brendan Hollis collection.

In an interview with NEW YORK TIMES reporters, Captain Frazer declared that on the night of the incident, he was on deck. He was knowledgeable of the reefs and had twenty years of experience running to Bermuda. "I looked for lights," he said, "and the mate looked for lights and the third mate looked for lights, and we could see no lights." Finally chief officer Williams saw a light and told the Captain he saw breakers about it. "The helm was put hard to starboard. I looked at the light and couldn't see any breakers. The light appeared to be fixed, so I decided it was the St. David's Head light, and ordered the ship steered east. In a few minutes she struck the reef. Captain Frazer went on to say that the light he saw was not St. David's Head, but Gibbs Hill light. Gibbs Hill light is a revolving light, but on this night, due to an accident, the reflectors had been replaced by tin, which frequently grew smokey causing the appearance of a fixed light.

The Marine Board of Inquiry found Captain Frazer negligent, but this ruling was later overturned in a British court.

This wreck was partially salvaged in WW II. Her engine is gone, but her twin boilers are still there and her stern overhangs into a sand hole. She sits in 25 feet of water on a hard coral bottom one mile from the *Caraquet* wreck which went down 20 years later in 1923. Visibility in the area is usually excellent averaging from 80 to 100 feet.

# MANILLA WRECK

The *Manilla Wreck* is the remains of a *Dutchman* wrecked in the northeast breakers. She lies east, one group of breakers away from the *Eagle* wreck,

Stacks of cannons on the *Manilla Wreck*. Photo by Alan Marquardt.

in 15 feet of water. The wreck seems to be lying upside down. Divers who visit the site will see stacks of cannons overgrown with coral. This unidentified wreck has been dated back to the mid 18th century.

# MARI CELESTE

Water color painting of the *Mari Celeste* sinking. Courtesy Mrs. Thomas Godet, Photo by Alan Marquardt.

## Mari Celeste

The *Mari Celeste* was a 207 ton, civil war blockade runner owned by the Crenshaw Brothers. The Confederate paddle wheel steamer which, according to the BERMUDA ROYAL GAZETTE, was known as "one of the swiftest and most fortunate of her class" had made at least five successful trips delivering goods into the south.

On September 13, 1846, under the command of Captain Sinclair and piloted by Bermudian, John Virgin, with a cargo of "classified merchandise", which included beef, bacon, ammunition and much needed rifles for the war effort, she left port enroute to Wilmington, North Carolina. The *Mari Celeste* made an unusually fast run through the east end channel and up the south side of the island. First officer Stuart announced some breakers he had spotted ahead, but the local pilot who was steerng the vessel replied "I know every rock here as well as I know my own house." Within moments, the vessel had slammed hard into the reef. She sank bow first within eight minutes. The ship's cook, who was the only casualty, had returned to his cabin against orders for some personal belongings and never made it out of the sinking ship.

The *Mari Celeste's* starboard side paddle wheel.
Photo by Michael Burke.

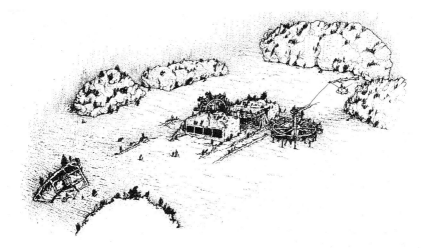

Sketch of the *Mari Celeste*. Courtesy Professor Gordon Watts, East Carolina University.

Today, the *Mari Celeste* sits in a sand hole in 55 feet of water about one half mile off the south coast of Bermuda. Her wreckage lies in a straight line with amidships being the highest wreckage left uncovered by sand. Divers can see and recognize both of her paddle wheels and her engine. Her bow section leans on its port side. This site is excellent for underwater photography especially when using the starboard side paddle wheel, which is standing upright, as a background.

# MARK ANTONIO

Wreck series postage stamp of the *Mark Antonio*. Courtesy Postmaster General.

The Spanish double ended mediterranean privateer, *Mark Antonio*, was on a voyage from St. Eustatius to Cape Henlopen, when she ran into Bermuda's reefs on July 18, 1777. According to the book SHIPWRECKS IN THE AMERICAS by Robert F. Marx, she was travelling in ballast under the command of Captain Jean Bautist Hugonne. Teddy Tucker discovered this wreck in the early 1960's. A few artifacts were found on her including musket shot and cannon balls. She now sits on a reef in 20 feet of water.

# MINERVA

Wreck series postage stamp of the *Minerva*. Courtesy Postmaster General.

This two masted sailing vessel pictured on one of Bermuda's Wreck Stamps was said to have sunk in 1849. After researching shipwrecks of Bermuda, we were able to locate very little information about this vessel. We did find reference to another *Minerva* which was sunk in 1795. She was on voyage from Norfolk, Virginia, to Tobago Island, under the command of Captain Arnet when she crashed into the reefs. According to Teddy Tucker, the *Minerva* has never been located, or if it has been found, it has never been positively identified. Mike Burke thinks that her wreckage may lie in Ely's Bay, but her true resting place may never be known.

# MINNIE BRESLAUER

The *Minnie Breslauer* was a 300 foot long English steamer under the command of Captain Peter Corbet. on January 1, 1873, the *Minnie Breslauer* set out on her maiden voyage, bound from Malaga to New York.

She ran aground on Bermuda's treacherous reefs. She was later pulled off the reef and towed but sunk enroute to St. Georges. All 24 crew members were rescued without mishap. According to Lloyds List, her cargo of fruit, cork, lead and wine was being salvaged from the wreck until March of the same year by B.W. Walker & Company.

Diver swims past the *Minnie Breslauer's* boiler.
Photo courtesy Alan Marquardt.

Denise Berg in the stern of the *Minnie Breslauer*.
Photo by Daniel Berg.

The *Minnie Breslauer* now sits on her port side in 50 to 65 feet of water off the south shore very close to Horseshoe Beach. Her bow sits all smashed up in the reef; amidships to her stern is semi-intact and rests on a sand sea bed. Her large single boiler and propeller are easily recognizable.

# *MONTANA*

This English paddle wheel steamer and civil war blockade runner was 236 feet long, had a 25 foot beam and displaced 750 tons. She was powered by 260 nhp twin oscillating cylinder engines. This vessel used at least three other names during her short life in an effort to elude the suspicions of Yankee spies; they were *Nola*, *Gloria*, and *Paramount*. On December 30, 1863, enroute from London to Wilmington, North Carolina, while carrying a cargo for the Confederacy and after completing the first leg of her dangerous maiden voyage across the stormy Atlantic, the *Montana*, sailing under the name *Nola*, attempted to enter Bermuda to take on coal. Under the command of Captain Pittman, she was wrecked near Western Blue Cut on Bermuda's reefs. A steam boat from St. George's went to her assistance and was able to save much of her cargo and crew, but could not pull her free from the reef due to a ten foot hole in her side.

*Montana's* paddle wheel. Photo by Peter Phillips.

Today, the scattered remains of the *Montana* or *Nola* lie in 30 feet of water eight miles northwest of Dockyard. Her bow is relatively intact, while her

Sketch of the *Montana*. Courtesy Professor Gordon Watts, East Carolina University.

engine stands upright with her two paddle wheels easily recognizable. Her stern section is slightly separated from the main wreckage. In the stern divers will find her elliptical fantail which is now heavily overgrown with coral. This wreck lies within swimming distance from the *Constellation* wreck, which crashed into the same reef in 1942.

# MUSSEL

According to Teddy Tucker's wreck map, the *Mussel* was a Bermuda double ended cedar fishing ketch which was wrecked on February 7, 1926, while returning from a fishing trip on the west end. Tragically, all hands were lost. She now sits in 25 feet of water on a sand bottom.

# NORTH CAROLINA

Wreck series postage stamp of the *North Carolina*. Courtesy Postmaster General.

The English iron barque, *North Carolina*, which was approximately 205 feet in length, was enroute from Bermuda to Liverpool, with a general cargo, including cotton and bark, when she struck a reef and sunk on January 1, 1880. According to the Board of Trade Casualty Returns 1879-83, the *North Carolina* was three years old, displaced 533 tons, was registered in Liverpool, owned by H. Barber and under the command of Captain Alexander Buchan. The Casualty Returns also tell us she was sunk 8.5 miles west and .5 miles south of Gibbs Hill Lighthouse.

On January 27, 1880, a salvage attempt was made to re-float the vessel. This attempt failed when the *North Carolina's* massive anchor broke free and crashed through the ship's hull.

Bowsprit of the *North Carolina*. Photo by Alan Marquardt.

Dead eyes are always a favorite subject for photographers who visit the *North Carolina*. Photo courtesy Michael Burke.

49

Today, the *North Carolina* sits upright in 25 to 45 feet of water. Her bow and stern are intact with her mid section collapsed. Her bowsprit and stern fantail and row of dead eyes all make excellent backgrounds for underwater photographers.

# H.M.S. PALLAS

Postage stamp of the *H.M.S. Pallas*. Courtesy Postmaster General.

The H.M.S. *Pallas* was wrecked in 1783. This 36 gun vessel under the command of Captain Christopher Parker ran aground off St. Georges Island. To date this wreck has not been discovered unless it is one of the unidentified ballast piles in the area.

# PELINAION

The Greek steamer, *Pelinaion*, was built in 1907 by Russell & Company, Port Glasgow, for Hill SS. Company, Ltd. and originally named *Hill Glen*. She was 385 feet in length, had a 49.9 foot beam, was powered by 384 n.p.h triple expansion engines and displaced 4,291 gross tons. In 1914, she was

The *K. Ktistakis* was sold and named *Pelinaion* in 1939. Courtesy William Schell, Photo by Paul Maya.

The Greek steamer *Pelinaion's* huge boiler. Photo courtesy Alan Marquardt.

The *Pelinaion* was 385 feet in length, had a 49.9 foot beam and was powered by 384 n.p.h. triple expansion engines. Today her engine stands upright and comes to within 10 feet of the surface. Photo courtesy Alan Marquardt.

sold and re-named *Doonholm*. After serving with a number of British tramp owners, she was sold in 1927 to G.K. Ktistakis, Chios, Greece, and renamed *K. Ktistakis*. In 1939, she was re-named once again the *Pelinaion*.

On December 22, 1939, the ship sailed from Takiradi, West Africa, for Baltimore, Maryland, with a cargo of iron ore. On January 16, 1939, under the command of Captain Janis Valikos, while heading for Bermuda to take on fuel, she was wrecked off David's Head, Bermuda. Captain Valikos was apparently unaware that St. David's Light was out due to the war, and he inaccurately calculated the position of his ship.

Today, the *Pelinaion* lies scattered in 65 feet of water. Her engine stands upright coming to within 10 feet of the surface, and her bow sits in only 20 feet of water. Mike Burke tells us of a tunnel like cave that starts on the reef, which allows divers to swim under the ship's hull and end up in her stern. Divers can see her deck winches, propeller and anchor while exploring this magnificent shipwreck.

# *POLLOCKSHIELDS*

Originally built as the *Herodot*, the *Pollockshields* was a 2,744 gross ton, 323 foot by 40 foot steamer that was powered by 281 n.h.p. triple expansion engines. She was built in 1890 by Reiherstieg Schiffswerft, Hamburg, for Deutsche Dampfs Ges. In 1903, she was sold to the Hamburg American Line and renamed *Graecia*. In 1904, World War I broke out, and this fine ship was outfitted as a German naval supply vessel. In August of 1914, she sailed from New York to the Azores. On October 10th of the same year, she was captured by the H.M.S. Argonaut. Taken over by the British Government, she was re-named *Pollockshields* and registered in the ownership of Tyack & Branfoot, Newcastle.

On August 22, 1915, with a crew of 37 and a cargo of 350 tons of ammunition including shells, gunpowder and provisions for WW I, the *Pollockshields* left Cardiff, Wales. On September 2nd, the steamer ran into a dense fog and hurricane force seas. By September 7, 1915, the fog lifted and as soon as the crew could see, they knew by the color of the water that they were in trouble. Ten minutes later, the ship struck a reef near Elbow Beach. According to the NEW YORK TIMES, all hands were mustered on the upper deck; life belts were given out, but they were one short. The captain sent boson Young below to get one. By this time, seas were sweeping over the deck making the job difficult. Young made it below only to find the doors locked. He got back and offered to go again if the Captain would give him the keys, but Captain Earnest Boothe said, "No boson that

Wreck of the *Pollockshields*. Photo courtesy Bermuda Archives.

Divers can still see live ammunition and shell casings. Photo by Peter Phillips.

The *Pollockshields* spare propeller. Photo by Peter Phillips.

Michael Burke holds shell casings recovered from the *Pollockshields*. Photo by Daniel Berg.

wouldn't be fair. You went down once, and now I will have a try.'' Captain Boothe was struck by a wall of water that swept him overboard. The last time anyone saw him alive was on top of a great sea within ten feet of a sharp coral reef. The rest of the crew reached shore safely later that day after the heroic efforts of life savers on the beach. Rescuers made five trips in a whaleboat through the heavy surf to take the crew ashore. The whole thrilling event was witnessed by guests of the Elbow Beach Hotel, then named South Shore Hotel.

For years, the *Pollockshields* engine protruded above the waves inviting tourists to swim out to her. So may of these swimmers were getting cut up on her coral covered wreckage that in 1960 the government hired Teddy Tucker to blow the legs off her engine. This took away the visual attraction and temptation of the wreck.

Today the wreck of the *Pollockshields* can be found scattered in 20 to 40 feet of water on a coral bottom. Loads of live ammunition and shell casings can be seen in amongst her wreckage. This wreck can be snorkeled to from the beach, but we recommend Scuba from a dive boat due to a powerful surge which is present on rough days.

# *RAMONA*

The Canadian steel hulled 120 foot long yacht, *Ramona*, was sunk on December 2, 1967. According to Teddy Tucker, she was under command

The Canadian steel hulled yacht *Ramona* was sunk on December 2, 1967. Only five of her crew of ten survived. Photo courtesy Mike Davis collection.

of Captain William Post McKay enroute from Lunenburg, Nova Scotia, to St. Lucia when the ship ran aground on a reef at 8:00 PM. Mike Davis reports that the crew of ten immediately sent up distress signals, but no one came to their aid. After abandoning ship in lifeboats, the wreck was finally noticed the next morning and reported to authorities. Many boats as well as aircraft rushed to help, but only five of the crew members survived the ordeal.

55

In the weeks following the accident, there was much speculation as to the competency of the *Ramona's* captain. It was reported that he was drunk during much of the voyage, an accusation which he strongly denied.

The *Ramona* was later raised with hopes of making the vessel sea worthy again, but it was discovered that such an undertaking was too extensive due to the damage incurred by her sinking. After salvaging everything of value from the *Ramona's* hull, she was sunk in a dump area off dockyard in 60 feet of water. Her bow now sits nestled inside the wreck of the *Dry Dock*, which was also scuttled on the same site.

# RICHARD P. BUCK

The 1,490 ton vessel, *Richard P. Buck*, was enroute from Philadelphia to San Fransisco under the command of Captain Carver. She had a 2,149 ton general cargo in her holds, which included kerosene and whiskey. On April 13, 1889, the vessel had encountered a violent storm, which caused extensive damage to her sails and rigging. After surviving the storm, the crew later discovered the ship to be on fire. Captain Carver immediately summoned help and the steam tug, Gladisfen, proceeded to her aid. The Gladisfen towed the *Buck* to shore, but by this time the rapidly spreading fire, fueled by her flammable cargo, had engulfed the entire ship. The BERMUDA ROYAL GAZETTE reported that "A very large number of spectators thronged the hills in the vicinity to witness the exciting, but sad spectacle, afforded by the brief destruction of so much valuable property."

Mike Davis reports that the burned remains of the *Richard P.Buck* can still be found off St. Georges. Divers will find some scattered wood beams and brass spikes on the site.

# SAN ANTONIO

The 300 ton Portuguese merchant nao *San Antonio*, was owned by Fernandino de Verar and under charter to the Spanish fleet. She was enroute from Cartagena to Cadiz with a cargo, according to Marx's book, SHIPWRECKS IN THE AMERICAS, "of 5,000 hides, 1,200 quintals of brazil wool, 6,000 pounds of indigo, 30,000 pounds of tobacco, 5,000 pounds of sarsaparilla," and 5,000 pounds of gold and silver and was armed with 12 cannons. The *San Antonio* was wrecked on the west reefs of Bermuda on September 12, 1621. Only 120 of her crew made it to shore. These survivors were soon beaten and tortured by local wreckers and forced to tell of the treasure the *San Antonio* had carried. Wreckers under the direction of Bermuda's Governor Butler recovered her anchors, four swivel guns, 11 cannons and almost all of her gold. Governor Butler left Bermuda on his own vessel shortly after the salvage operation, before his term was over. Suspicion has always been that he made off with the treasure.

In 1960, Teddy Tucker spotted something in a sand pocket while on a fishing trip. He made a quick dive and found a cannon. Immediately he knew he had found yet another shipwreck. Together with Peter Stackpole and Robert Canton, he worked the 20 foot deep wreck site. Together they recovered pieces of pottery, musket shot, coins, a gold chain, navigational dividers, swords and an emerald mounted ring.

# SAN PEDRO

Wreck series postage stamp of the *San Pedro*. Courtesy Postmaster General.

The 350 ton, Spanish nao *San Pedro*, was part of the Nueva Espana Flota on a voyage from Cartagena to Cadiz and under the command of Captain Hieronimo de Porras when she was wrecked in November of 1596.

In 1951, while looking for some lost fish traps, Teddy Tucker, spotted some cannons sitting on the seabed 30 feet below. Tucker raised the cannons, which were later sold to the government. For a while the site was referred to as *Old Spaniard*. Tucker realized his find was old but because of other projects didn't return to work the site for five years. He returned with Robert Canton and started to dig in the sand. What they found, according to Mark, in his book SHIPWRECKS IN THE AMERICAS, was the first major treasure recovery of the twentieth century. Within weeks, Tucker had found a 32 ounce gold bar, two small gold cakes and an emerald studded gold crucifix. By the time their work was finished, they had recovered a bronze mortar dated 1561, a gold bar plus countless other treasures including navigating instruments, pewter, tools, ceramic utensils, 2,000 silver coins, six pearl studded gold buttons, and rare Carib Indian weapons. The minted date of the latest coin was 1592. Mendel Peterson, in his book, HISTORY UNDER THE SEA, refers to Tucker's artifacts as the "Most significant Tudor period find of this century." On the site, which Tucker and Canton located in 1951, no absolute positive identification has been found to determine the ship's true identity. All artifacts and research point to the ship being the *San Pedro*. The *San Pedro* was listed on documents

Teddy Tucker found his famous Tucker emerald studded cross on the wreck of the 350 ton Spanish nao *San Pedro*. The *San Pedro* was sunk on September 12, 1621. Photo by Alan Marquardt.

Teddy Tucker holds some coins he recovered from the *San Pedro*. Photo by Daniel Berg.

at Madrid and Seville as being "Lost at Bermuda." The date fits Teddy's wreck, and her anchor and iron cannons indicate a merchant vessel rather than a galleon.

Years later, the famous Tucker emerald studded cross was stolen. At the time it was on display at the Aquarium museum. The theft was only discovered when Teddy Tucker went to select items to be displayed for the Queen's visit at the opening of the Maritime Museum in Dockyard. The thief had replaced the cross with a cheap plastic replica, and to this date the treasure has not been seen again.

This site is in a sand hole in only 15 to 30 feet of water. All that remains exposed are some timbers and a ballast pile.

## SANTA ANA

The Spanish nao *Santa Ana*, was a merchant vessel on a voyage from Honduras to Cadiz, Spain, when she was wrecked in 1605. At the time, she was carrying a general cargo that included exotic woods.

The wreck known as *Santa Ana* now sits in 12 feet of water off the west end. She has never been positively identified but is assumed to be the *Santa Ana*.

## SEA VENTURE

The English flagship, *Sea Venture*, under the command of Admiral Sir George Somers, was leading a squadron of ships from Plymouth, England,

Wreck of the *Sea Venture*. Drawing courtesy THIS WEEK IN BERMUDA Magazine.

Statue of Admiral Sir George Somers whose shipwrecked vessel *Sea Venture* brought Bermuda's first colonists.

A full size replica of the Deliverance in St Georges. The Deliverance was built by the Sea Ventures shipwrecked crew so they could continue there journey to the New World. Photo by Dainel Berg.

to Jamestown, Virginia, with settlers and supplies for the new colony. On July 25, 1609, a hurricane blew the *Sea Venture* off course. Three days later, on July 28th, after having suffered severe damage from the storm, the crew was grateful to spot land. Admiral Somers grounded the ship a half mile off St. Catherine's point. Fortunately all 150 passengers and crew were able to make it to land bringing much of the *Sea Venture's* cargo with them. Within a short time, the *Sea Venture* broke up and sank.

These castaways were Bermuda's first settlers. The settlers built two small vessels named the Deliverance and the Patience. In May of 1610, all but three men sailed to Jamestown on these improvised sailing vessels. On arrival they found only 60 survivors out of the 500 settlers left in Jamestown the previous year. Indian attacks and poor crops had plagued the Jamestown colony. Admiral Somers returned to Bermuda and died on the island he had come to love. His heart and entrails are buried in St. George, while his body was returned to England.

In June of 1958, Edmund Downing set out to find the *Sea Ventures* remains. Research told him that the wreck lay in an area named Sea Venture Shoal. In October of the same year, Downing found a wreck in 30 feet of water. The Smithsonian's, Mendel Peterson, and local shipwreck authority, Teddy Tucker, were called in to make a positive identification of the site. After unearthing a stone jug, clay pipe, and a vase of the correct period and taking timber measurements, they concluded that this was indeed the vessel that had brought Bermuda's first colonists.

## *TAUNTON*

The *Taunton's* engine. Photo by
Michael Burke.

Wreck of the *Taunton*. Photo by
Michael Burke.

Alan Marquardt holds the bell
Teddy Tucker recovered from the
*Taunton*.

The Norwegian cargo steamer, *Taunton*, built in 1902 by Burmeister & Wain, Copenhagen, was owned by A.F. Kaceness & Company. She was 228.5 feet in length, had a 32.6 foot beam and displaced 1,329 gross tons. She was powered by a triple expansion engine.

On November 24, 1920, the *Taunton* was wrecked on Bermuda's northern reefs. At the time, she was enroute from Norfolk, Virginia, to St. George, with a cargo of coal. She was under the command of Captain Olsen and sailing through a misty fog when she hit the reef.

Today, the *Taunton* rests in 20 feet of water on the northeast reef. Her wreckage is broken up and scattered, but her engine and boilers still stand upright. An interesting side story to this wreck is that Teddy Tucker found and recovered the ship's bell. The bell was later used as a prop in the movie, THE DEEP. The *Taunton's* bell can now be seen in the Gibbs Hill lighthouse museum.

# *TRITON FERRY*

The 65 foot ferry *Triton* was scuttled in May of 1988. Photos courtesy Alan Marquardt.

The 65 foot ferry *Triton* was scuttled in May, 1988, approximately seven miles off the southwest side of the island, as a dive site by the Bermuda Divers Association (BDA). Before her sinking, great care was taken to clean her and make her safe for divers. Ian Murdoch sent us a sketch of the *Triton's* engine room plaque. The plaque read, "Built and Engined by Brookes Marine Ltd., Shipbuilders & Engineers, Lowestoft 1960." At the time of this printing, the *Triton* has yet to be located. According to Mike Burke, she should be sitting in about 55 to 80 feet of water and once found will make a good dive site.

# *VIRGINIA MERCHANT*

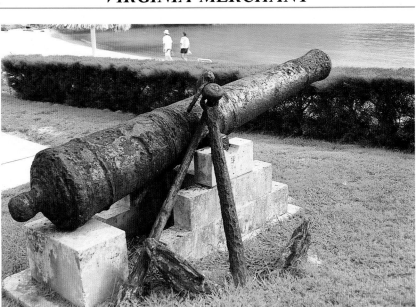

A cannon salvaged from the area of the *Virginia Merchant*. Photo by Daniel Berg.

The *Virginia Merchant* was an English vessel owned by the Virginia Company and bound from Plymouth, England, to Jamestown, Virginia, carrying 179 passengers and a general cargo. On March 26, 1661, under the command of Captain Robert Burke, the *Virginia Merchant* left Castle Harbor. Captain Burke soon found his vessel being ripped apart on a shallow reef only 250 yards from shore. Only ten of the passengers and crew managed to survive the ordeal.

The *Virginia Merchant* was discovered by treasure hunter, Teddy Tucker. Tucker's find was of great archaeological interest because he found a sheathing of animal hair attached to the exterior of the *Virginia Merchant's* hull. This was done in earlier times in an attempt to protect the wood from wood eating worms (teredos). To date there are only one or two other known examples of animal hair sheathing ever found on a shipwreck. One example was found on the unidentified ballast pile in Florida known as the Wedge Wreck.

Today, the wreck sits in 12 to 45 feet of water. Part of her wreckage lie outside and part inside the breakers off Sonesta Beach. All that divers will see at this site are her anchor, small ballast pile and some wood debris. A cannon that was salvaged from the area of the *Virginia Merchant* wreck is mounted with a plaque by the beach at Sonesta Beach Hotel.

# H.M.S. VIXEN

Wreck series postage stamp of the *H.M.S. Vixen*. Courtesy Postmaster General.

The gunboat *H.M.S. Vixen* displaced 1,230 tons and was built by Lungley Shipyard, Deptford, England, in 1864, and launched in 1867. According to Professor Richard Gould of Brown University in Providence, Rhode Island, the *Vixen* was the first twin-screwed vessel of the Royal Navy. *Vixen's* iron hull was completely clad in teak wood. This design was made in an effort to overcome problems that iron hulled ships were having with marine organisms. The teak also produced extra drag on the ship, therefore, resulting in the *Vixen* being the slowest ironclad vessel in the Royal Navy. Another very interesting aspect of this ship is that she was built with a ram type bow. Her heavily supported bow protruded forward almost nine feet under the water line. Unfortunately, after sea trials, the *Vixen* and her sister ship, Viper, were considered too slow as well as unseaworthy. They were withdrawn from service in 1887 and towed to Bermuda in 1888 as coast defense ships. By 1895, *Vixen* had been allocated as a floating dormitory to house Dockyard laborers. In 1896, after removal of her engines and machinery, she was scuttled to block a narrow channel off Daniel's Head. This scuttling was done to prevent possible attacks by torpedo boats on Dockyard.

In 1986, Professor Richard Gould, along with Earthwatch and the Bermuda Maritime Museum, began a three year project that researched the vessel and produced fine underwater sketches of the site. In 1987, probably due to publicity from Professor Gould's activity, an official *Vixen* postage stamp was issued, and the site was classified as a protected wreck. This means that

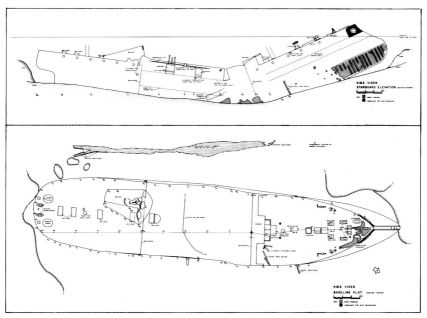

Underwater sketches of the *H.M.S. Vixen*. Courtesy Professor Richard Gould.

The *H.M.S. Vixen* was the first twin-screwed vessel of the Royal navy. Her bow protrudes through the oceans surface. Photo by Daniel Berg.

nothing can be removed from the wreck, and a permit is needed to explore the *Vixen* while on SCUBA although no permit is needed to snorkel the site.

Today, the *Vixen* is a popular site for glass bottom boats. Her bow protrudes above the water line, and her hull is almost completely intact.

# WARWICK

Wreck series postage stamp of the *Warwick*. Courtesy Postmaster General.

The English merchantman, *Warwick*, was owned by the Earl of Warwick and on charter to the Virginia Company when she was sunk by a strong gale in Castle Harbor in November of 1619. Fortunately, all passengers had disembarked, and her cargo was removed before the storm that sank her hit. After sinking, the wreck was quickly engulfed in the bay's silt, which preserved the wood and prevented teredos (wood eating worms) from getting to her. This wreck was discovered with the use of a magnetometer by Mendel Peterson and Teddy Tucker in 1967. When found it represented the most complete wooden hulled English merchantmen discovered to that date.

# WYCHWOOD

The English Steamer *Wychwood*. Photo courtesy Mike Davis collection.

The English steamer *Wychwood* was built in 1950 by S.P. Austin & Son, Ltd., Sunderland, England, for Wm. France Fenwick & Company, Ltd., London. She was 302.5 feet in length, had a 45 foot beam and displaced 2,506 gross tons.

At 8:35 PM on August 11, 1955, while enroute from Walton, Nova Scotia, to Port of Spain, Trinidad, with a cargo of barytes, the *Wychwood* ran aground in 18 feet of water ten miles from Gibbs Hill Light. According to Lloyds Weekly Casualty Reports, the *Wychwood* was finally pulled off and re-floated by the United States Navy tug, Papago, and the Coast Guard cutter, Rockaway, on August 12th. At that time, she was leaking badly, but her pumps were handling the flooding without too much trouble. They started to tow her stern first because her rudder had been damaged towards St. Georges. On August 13th, the *Wychwood* was anchored at Five Fathom's Hole and abandoned due to the heavy weather from the approaching hurricane, Diane. The crew was transferred to the cutter, Rockaway. On August 14th, 11:50 AM, it was reported that the *Wychwood* sank in 50 to 60 feet of water after her pumps could no longer keep up with the influx of rushing sea water. Only the tips of her masts remained above the water.

The Marine Court of Inquiry concluded that the stranding was primarily caused by the negligence of her master.

The *Wychwood* was later blown up because she was a hazard to navigation, and she now lies scattered across the ocean floor.

# ZOVETTO

*Zovetto* wreckage. Photo by Alan Marquardt.

## *Zovetto*

The Cargo steamer *Zovetto* was built in 1919 by A. Stephen & Sons, Ltd., Glasgow. Originally named, *War Gascon*, she was 399.6 feet in length, 52.4 feet wide and displaced 5,107 gross tons. She was originally going to be completed as a tanker with the installation of tanks in her cargo holds, but due to the end of the war, was completed as a dry cargo "A" type standard tramp. She was sold to Parodi & Accame, Genoa, and re-named *Zovetto*.

On February 13, 1924, the Italian steamship, *Zovetto*, enroute from Poti on the Black Sea to Baltimore, Maryland, with a load of manganese ore ran aground off St. David's Light. Captain Fortunat de Gregant was being lead by a Bermudian pilot boat. Apparently due to bad weather, he somehow ended up on the wrong side and missed the channel. No lives were lost, and the *Zovetto's* cargo was later salvaged.

Today, this wreck is also known as *Rita Zovetto* or *Zovetta*. She lies in 20 to 70 feet of water outside the breakers on the east end of the island close to the wreck of the *Pelinaion*.

# INDEX

# DIVE OPERATIONS

BLUE WATER DIVERS
Robinson's Marina
Somerset Bridge, Bermuda
(809) 234-1034

DIVE BERMUDA
6 Dockyard Terrace
Ireland Island, Bermuda
(809) 234-0225

NAUTILUS DIVING, LTD.
Po Box HM 237
Southampton Princess
Hamilton, Bermuda HM AX
(809) 238-2332
(809) 238-8000

SOUTH SIDE SCUBA, LTD.
Po Box PG 38
Pag, Bermuda PG BX
(Grotto Bay Hotel)
(809) 293-2915
(Sonesta Beach Hotel)
(809) 238-1822

BRONSON HARTLEY'S HELMET DIVING
(809) 292-4434

GREG HARTLEY'S HELMET DIVING
(809) 234-2861

JESSIE JAMES SNORKELING
(809) 236-4804

Send For Our
**FREE**
Catalog of Dive Publications
*Aqua Explorers, Inc.*
*Po Box 116*
*East Rockaway, NY 11518*
Phone/Fax (516) 868-2658